بسم الله الرحمن الرحيم

ALLAH´S NAME I BEGIN WITH,

THE MOST MERCIFUL

THE MOST COMPASSIONATE

FIRST EDITION

ISBN: 978-0-9571096-2-9

Title: **The Four Sources of Sharī'ah - an Introduction to *Usūl al-Fiqh***
Author: **Dr. Hāfiz Ather Hussain al-Azharī**

Published by **Abul Noor Publications,**
Leicester, United Kingdom

Website: **www.abulnoor.com**
Email: **publications@abulnoor.com**

Cover design by Zain ul-Abedin (Faadil)

Designed, printed & bound in the
United Kingdom by OUTSTANDING
Email: books@standoutnow.co.uk
Tel: +44 (0)121 327 3277

THE FOUR SOURCES OF SHARI‘AH.

WRITTEN BY
Dr Hafiz Ather Hussain al-Azhari

اللهمّ صلّ وسلّم وبارك على سيّدنا
محمّدٍ عددَ ما صلّيتَ وسلّمتَ و
باركتَ عليه أنت وملائكتُكَ

For the *Isaal Sawab* of
Hafiz Mahboob Hussain al-Azhari's late mother
Taslim Begum (d. 2017).

May Allah shower her grave
with mercy and blessings.

Ameen

CONTENTS

ACKNOWLEDGEMENTS

My sincerest thanks goes to my family, friends and colleagues who have helped me every step of the way in this project. In particular, I would like to thank Hafiz Gul Muhammad (Jamia al-Karam), Allama Asif Ali al-Azhari, Shahid Hussain, Yassir Hussain, Aisha Hussain, Bilal Ahmed Choudhry, Hafiz Muhammad Khizar (Ghamkol Sharif), Taahir Patel, Zain ul-Abedeen Patel, Hafiza Rahiela Ayub Ashrafi, Hafiz Zakeer Patel, Yaseen Karatela, Waqas Rafiq, Raza Sakhi (Solicitor-Advocate) and Dr Mohammad Afraz Ahmed, who all sacrificed their precious time in order to check the drafts and offer brilliant advice. Finally, I would like to thank the wonderful Faadil (Zain ul-Abedin) of *Outstanding*, for his creative input into the design and print of this book. May Allah reward them all for their dedication and passion for Islam, *āmīn*.

ABOUT THE AUTHOR

Dr. Hafiz Ather Hussain al-Azhari is an Imam, writer and researcher.

Ather Hussain began his Islamic education by completing the memorisation of the Holy Qur'ān at the age of thirteen. After completing his GCSEs he moved to Jāmia al-Karam, where he studied Arabic Grammar & Islamic Studies under the guardianship of Shaykh Muhammad Imdād Hussain Pirzāda and Mawlāna Abdul-Bārī Sahib. In 1995, he travelled to Bhera Sharīf in Pakistan, and completed the traditional seminary course with First Class Honours. Here he had the opportunity to be taught directly by Ziā al-Ummah Pīr Muhammad Karam Shāh al-Azharī (may Allāh shower His mercy upon him).

Between 1996 and 1999, he studied at al-Azhar University in Cairo, the oldest seat of Islamic learning in the world. He specialised in Hadīth Studies, and graduated in BA Principles of Theology in 1999.

Upon returning to England, he joined the University of Birmingham to study BA Political Science, and he graduated with First Class Honours in 2003. In 2006, he completed his MPhil in Theology on the *al-Jāmī* of al-Khatīb al-Baghdādī and in 2012, he completed his PhD in Theology (on the *Nuzha* of Ibn Hajar al-Asqalānī), all at the same university.

He has translated several Islamic texts from Urdu to English, most notably *Tafseer Imdād al-Karam* (volume one), by M.I.H. Pirzāda and *Sūrah al-Fātiha* by Allāma Ghulām Rasūl Saī'dī. In collaboration with Dr. Allāma Muhammad Shāhid Razā Na'īmī OBE, he has also written *Towards Understanding Aqidah*, *Imam Hussain & the Tragedy of Karbala* and *Al-Isra wa'l Mi'raj - An Account of the Miraculous Night Journey of our Beloved Prophet*ﷺ . Most recently (January 2016), he edited *Ghibtat al-Nāzir fī Tarjamat al-Shaykh Abd al-Qādir* (The Onlooker's Delight Concerning the Biography of al-Shaykh Abd al-Qādir).

Dr. Hafiz Ather Hussain lives in Leicester with his wife and three daughters, Aisha, Aarifa and Aaliya.

FOREWORD

Allāh's name I begin with, the Most-Merciful, the Most-Compassionate. All praise is for Allāh, the Master, the Most Exalted and the Most High. And salutations and blessings be upon our leader, Sayyidunā Muhammad ﷺ, his family and his Companions.

Dr. Hafiz Ather Hussain al-Azhari has completed an outstanding work on the sources of Sharī'ah (Islamic Law) - namely the Qur'ān, Sunnah, *Ijmā* and *Qiyās* - and kindly requested me to provide the foreword for it. Upon reading it carefully, I found it to be presented in very simple English. I congratulate Hafiz Ather on producing a highly educational work, presented in an accessible manner. Undoubtedly, the book will be an ideal gift for the young Muslims of the West, as well as individuals who take a real interest in studying Islām. Supported with evidence and references, this guide will provide readers with a clear window to understanding the four sources of Sharī'ah.

I have known Hafiz Ather since his childhood. He has always shown simplicity and contentment in his life and in his works. On behalf of *Markazī Ulamā Council* (UK), *Jamā'at Ahl al-Sunna* (UK) and the Muslims of Leicester, I sincerely congratulate him on his efforts. I pray to Allāh Almighty to accept this work and to bless him with further success in propagating Islām, *āmīn*.

Imām al-Millat Imām Hāfiz Hafeez al-Rahmān Chishtī
Imām at Jāmia Masjid Bilāl, Leicester

AUTHOR'S FOREWORD

All praise is for Allāh, Lord of the Worlds. And salutations and blessings be upon the best of all creations, Sayyidunā Muhammad ﷺ and his family.

Usūl al-Fiqh deals with how rules and regulations are derived from the four principal sources of Islamic Sharī'ah, namely the Qur'ān, Sunnah (the Prophetic example), *Ijmā* (scholarly consensus) and *Qiyās* (analogy). This topic is important in this day and age for various reasons:

a. The reappearance of *Ghayr Muqallids*.[1] The *madhhab* system is under attack from extremists like Daesh, who have taken law-making into their own hands. For example, in February 2015, Daesh burned the Jordanian Muslim pilot Moaz al-Kasasbeh alive. They erroneously argued that this was in line with the teachings of Islām, citing the report of Sayyidunā Alī (may Allāh be pleased with him)

1 This term refers to the Muslims who do not adhere to the main, judicial schools of thought of Imām Abū Hanīfa, Imām Mālik, Imām al-Shāfi'ī and Imām Ahmad ibn Hanbal.

who reportedly punished someone in this manner. This report is to be found in *Sahīh al-Bukhārī*.[2] If Daesh had any real knowledge of *Usūl al-Fiqh*, they would know that this report is by no means support for burning Muslims alive. No Islamic scholar has ever allowed the practice based on this report. Despite this, Daesh have ignorantly approved it. In a similar manner, they have destroyed the shrines of the pious Muslims (including prophets) and again sought to justify it from the Sunnah.

Extremists follow their own egoistic agenda and then try to seek justification from Sharī'ah. As they do so, they totally ignore the rich heritage of Islamic scholarship. True Muslims can only identify the misdemeanours of such groups and subsequently refute them if they understand how *Usūl al-Fiqh* works.

b. The devaluation of Islamic scholarship. With the appearance of English translations for countless Islamic scriptures and classics, there has been a surge of young people who have taken an interest in Islamic scholarship, but have little or no

2 *Sahīh al-Bukhārī, Kitāb istitāba al-murtaddīn wa'l mu'ānidin wa qitāluhum*). Ikrama reports that some atheists were brought to Alī and he burnt them. The news of the event reached Ibn Abbās (may Allāh be pleased with them) who said, 'If I had been in his place, I would not have burned them, as Allāh's Messenger ﷺ forbade it, saying 'Do not punish anybody with Allāh's punishment.'

interest in studying it full time under a experienced teacher. The result is that they often make critical mistakes in their judgement of Qur'ānic verses, prophetic reports and the opinions of scholars. This book aims to show that giving an opinion on Islamic matters is a very weighty matter and should be approached with caution.

c. The appearance of reformist Muslims. Whenever Muslims faced calamities, oppression and misfortunes in the past, they always re-examined themselves. After all, Allāh only changes a community when they strive to change themselves (Qur'ān, 13:11). Unfortunately, there is a growing voice in the Muslim community today who believe Islām is the problem, not Muslims. They advocate that Islām has not evolved fast enough to keep up with the trends of the twenty-first century and as a result, Muslims are facing turmoil and strife. The reality is that these same Muslims know very little about what Sharī'ah is, how it works and how flexible it is. Had they studied *Usūl al-Fiqh* in detail, they would realise that Islām is fit for every Muslim, in every era and region. Muslims have to change, not Islām.

I hope this book will give a sound introduction to *Usūl al-Fiqh* for readers of all ages. This book is not a detailed guide to *Usūl al-Fiqh*, which is otherwise a subject area that is complicated and something that is taught very late on in the Islamic scholarship programme. Rather, it is a simple taster of how intrinsic, wonderful and complex Sharī'ah is.

This book is the result of a four-week course that was delivered in November 2015 at Jāmia Masjid Bilāl, Leicester. My thanks to the management committee of this mosque and its Imām, Qārī Hafeez al-Rahmān Chishtī, for inviting me to deliver the course there.

The commendable parts of this work are due to Allāh's limitless favour and mercy. The shortcomings are all my own.

Finally, I request the readers to remember my family in their supplications. May Allāh forgive our sins and grant us bliss in both worlds, *āmīn*.

Dr. Hafiz Ather Hussain al-Azhari

@hafiz_ather

BA Principles of Theology, al-Azhar University, Cairo, Egypt

MA Arabic and Islamic Studies, Dar al-Ulum Muhammadia Ghawsia, Bhera, Pakistan.

BA Political Science, MPhil Theology & PhD Theology, University of Birmingham.

1.0. INTRODUCTION

1.1. What are the four sources of Sharīʿah?

Sharī'ah means the law and constitution of Islām for Muslims. It is the means by which a Muslim can achieve the ultimate goal in life, namely following the footsteps of Prophet Muhammad ﷺ. The four sources of Sharī'ah are (i) the Qur'ān (ii) the Sunnah (iii) *Ijmā* (iv) *Qiyās*. Of these four, the Qur'ān and Sunnah are the true, primary sources of Sharī'ah. What this means is that although there are four sources, *Ijmā* and *Qiyās* are still dependent on the Qur'ān and Sunnah. *Qiyās* cannot be done outside the prism of the Qur'ān and Sunnah. Likewise, any *Ijmā* that is contrary to the Qur'ān and Sunnah is not a consensus of any value. The Holy Qur'ān states:

يٰأيها الَّذِينَ اٰمَنُوا اَطِيْعُوا اللّٰهَ وَاَطِيْعُوا الرسولَ وَأُولِي الاَمْرِ مِنْكُمْ

O those who believe! Obey Allāh and obey the Messenger and those who are in authority amongst you.

(Qur'ān, 4:59)

This verse orders Muslims to show obedience to Allāh, His Messenger ﷺ and the people of authority. Importantly, the verb 'obey' features before 'Allāh' and before the 'Messenger', but not before the 'people of authority'.[3] The reason for this is that obedience to the people of authority is dependent on their obedience to the Allah and His Messenger. If they do not legislate according to the framework of the Qur'ān and Sunnah, then their opinion is not considered.

It is also important to note that Sharī'ah is only applicable to Muslims. That is why in the Holy Qur'ān, the order to perform *ṣalāh* (prayer) commences with 'O those who believe' as opposed to 'O Mankind'. It is strange that many extremists try to preach practical matters pertaining to Sharī'ah to the non-Muslims in the UK (non-Muslims should refrain from alcohol, for example), not realising it is not incumbent upon them until they accept Islām.

This book will devote one chapter to each of the sources of Sharī'ah, commencing with the miraculous and divine Qur'ān.

3 The verse reads 'Obey Allāh and obey the Messenger and the people of authority' and it does not read 'Obey Allāh and obey the Messenger and obey the people of authority.'

2.0. THE HOLY QUR'ĀN

2.1. Introduction

The Holy Qur'ān is the word of Allāh, revealed to mankind via the means of Prophet Muhammadﷺ. The Qur'ān is unbelievably simple yet complex. There is something to be gained from it for each and every person. It is simple enough for a young child to learn and take joy from it, and yet complex enough to baffle the most learned of men. The Arabs were astonished by it as were the philosophers. The scientists marvel at it as do the mathematicians. In short, the Qur'ān leaves a lasting impression on everyone.

In many places, the Qur'ān affirms that it is an explanation for all things:

وَنَزَّلْنَا عَلَيْكَ الْكِتَابَ تِبْيَانًا لِكُلِّ شَيْءٍ وَهُدًى وَرَحْمَةً وَبُشْرَىٰ لِلْمُسْلِمِينَ

And We have sent down to you the Qur'ān
as an explanation of everything, a guidance,
a mercy and glad tidings for Muslims

(Qur'ān, 16: 89).

This chapter will not talk about the perfect nature of the Qur'ān and its everlasting miracle. Instead, it will concentrate on the Qur'ān's role in Sharī'ah.

Generally speaking, it is the *Madanī* verses that make up Sharī'ah, rather than the *Makkī* ones.[4] Whereas *Makkī* verses refer to *tawhīd*, the evil nature of idol-worship, belief in the angels and scriptures, *Madanī* verses are relatively longer and include specific directives on how to live together.

It is said that there are about five hundred Qur'ānic verses that have direct legal significance. Importantly however, none of the verses in the Qur'ān can be said to be purely legal; they are always coupled with the spiritual and moral. That is why many of these verses conclude with Allāh telling us He is the *Khabīr* (the All-Knowing) and the *Basīr* (the All-Seeing). The verse that outlines Islamic inheritance also reminds us that Allah is All-Knowing and Wise (Qur'ān,4: 11). The same verse that instructs Muslims to fast also refers to *taqwā* (God-consciousness) (Qur'ān, 2: 183). In other words, Sharī'ah is aimed at human betterment, both inwardly and outwardly.

4 A *Makkī* verse or chapter is one that was revealed before the Prophet's ﷺ Migration to al-Madīna and a *Madanī* verse or chapter is one that was revealed after the Prophet's ﷺ Migration to al-Madīna.

2.2. The complexity of the Qur'ān

In terms of its validity, authenticity and transmission from the Prophet ﷺ, the Qur'ān is definitive and incontrovertible. In terms of its meaning as far as we are concerned, there are two categories:

(i) verses that are definitive in their meaning.

(ii) verses that are open to interpretation.

An example of each will be given below.

2.2.1. For example, Allāh says in the Qur'ān:

لَا يُؤَاخِذُكُمُ اللَّهُ بِاللَّغْوِ فِي أَيْمَانِكُمْ وَلَٰكِن يُؤَاخِذُكُم بِمَا عَقَّدتُّمُ
الْأَيْمَانَ فَكَفَّارَتُهُ إِطْعَامُ عَشَرَةِ مَسَاكِينَ مِنْ أَوْسَطِ مَا تُطْعِمُونَ
أَهْلِيكُمْ أَوْ كِسْوَتُهُمْ أَوْ تَحْرِيرُ رَقَبَةٍ فَمَن لَّمْ يَجِدْ فَصِيَامُ ثَلَاثَةِ أَيَّامٍ

Allāh will not hold you responsible for what is unintentional in your oaths, but He will hold you responsible for your deliberate oaths; for its expiation, feed ten poor people, on a scale of the average of that with which you feed your own families, or clothe them or free a slave. But whosoever cannot afford that, then he should fast for three days

(Qur'ān, 5: 89).

This verse indicates what a Muslim should do when he deliberately breaks an oath, either feed or clothe ten people, free a slave or fast for three days. In this verse, 'ten' and 'three' are definitive words and are clear in the message it aims to portray. It cannot mean anything else. This, therefore, requires little deliberation and thought.

2.2.2. Compare this now with the following verse, one that is open to interpretation:

وَالْمُطَلَّقَاتُ يَتَرَبَّصْنَ بِأَنْفُسِهِنَّ ثَلَاثَةَ قُرُوءٍ

And divorced women shall wait for three qurū

(Qur'ān, 2:228).

The word *qurū* (قروء) here can mean two things; the menstrual period of a woman or the period when she is free from menstruation. Hence, Muslim scholars with an expertise in Islām and Arabic are required to interpret such verses.

2.2.3. In fact, even the simplest of words must be carefully addressed in the Holy Qur'ān. For instance, the word *ilā* (الي) generally means 'up to'. In the following verse, ilā means 'up to *and* inclusive of':

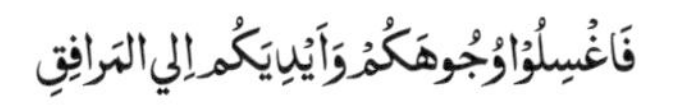

So wash your faces and your hands
up to [and including] the elbows

(Qur'ān, 5:6).

In other words, in ablution Muslims wash the arms to the elbows, meaning the elbow is inclusive. However, elsewhere in the Qur'ān, ilā means 'up to' only:

ثُمَّ أَتِمُّوا الصِّيَامَ اِلَى اللَّيْلِ

Then complete the fast up to the nightfall

(Qur'ān, 2:187).

Here, the order is to complete the fast until the night, meaning up to and not inclusive. So even a simple word like *ilā* has many meanings. It is the scholars who have analysed such words and provided rules and maxims for deducing what each letter means and in which context.[5]

In order to aid understanding of such complexities, the learned scholars have analysed the words and verses according to type and meaning. Each type then has its own definition, principle and ruling. Some of the terminologies introduced by scholars of *Usūl al-Fiqh* to understand the Qur'ān and Sunnah include:

- *Khās* (particular) and *Āmm* (universal)
- *Haqīqat* (literal) and *Majāz* (figurative)
- *Mutlaq* (unqualified phrases) and *Muqayyad* (qualified phrases)
- *Mujmal* (ambiguous) and *Mubayyan* (clarified)
- *Nāsikh* (abrogating) and *Mansūkh* (abrogated)
- *Amr* (commands) and *Nahi* (prohibitions)

5 The linguists have stated that with regards to *ilā* (إلى), they have stated that if what appears before and after *ilā* is from the same genus, then *ilā* is inclusive. But if what appears before and after *ilā* is not from the same genus, then *ilā* simply means 'up to' and not inclusive. The *Usūl* scholars write that if *ilā* is used for *imtidād* (extending a limited task) then it means 'up to'. If *ilā* is used for *isqāt* (restricting an unlimited task), then it means 'up to and including'.

These simple examples show that the rules of Sharī'ah that are derived from the Qur'ān require careful deliberation and research. The depth and complexity of the terms means it is not permissible for an unqualified person to make a judgement on the Qur'ān without first studying *Usūl al-Fiqh*. In fact, the Prophet ﷺ warned Muslims not to give an opinion on the Qur'ān without the necessary skills. He said:

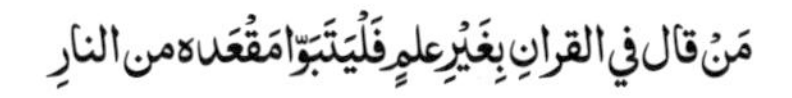

Whosoever speaks regarding the Qur'ān with his own opinion [alone], then let him prepare his abode in the fire.[6]

Because some 'scholars' have no training in Islamic theology, they have made blatant errors in translating and understanding the Qur'ān. For instance, some have translated the word al-*Ummī* (when describing Prophet Muhammad ﷺ) from the

6 *Musnad Ahmad ibn Hanbal*, Musnad Banī Hāshim; Musnad Abd Allāh ibn Abbās ibn Abd al-Muttalib.

Qur'ān in an insulting and wholly inaccurate manner.[7] One should not give an opinion on the Qur'ān if one is not educated. Instead, leave it to the specialists.

2.3. The vastness of the Qur'ān

If a Muslim can demonstrate proficiency in understanding the meanings of the Qur'ān (and the corresponding *Usūl al-Fiqh* terminologies), then the prize is astonishing. It opens up a window to appreciate the words of Allāh and to derive countless rulings from each verse.

The richness of the Qur'ān is evident in the works of the skilled scholars who were able to derive rulings and pearls of wisdom from *sūrahs*, verses and even individual words. Sayyiduna Alī

7 Many modern 'scholars' have translated *al-Ummī* as 'illiterate' (God forbid). Ibn Manzūr writes that *umm* means the essence and origin of something. *Sūrah al-Fātihah* is called *umm al-kitāb* because it is considered the root and essence of the Qur'ān. Alcohol is called *umm al-khabā'ith* because it is considered the root of all evil. On this basis, Prophet Muhammad ﷺ is called al-Ummī because he is the root of all existence. Others write that that Prophet Muhammad was born in Makka, also known as *Umm al-Qurā* (the mother of all cities). Thus, his title of *al-Ummī* is a reference to Makka. Imām al-Sha'rāwī offers a beautiful definition of *al-Ummī* when he writes 'one taught directly by Allāh alone with no human intervention.' None of the great learned scholars from the past translated *al-Ummī* as illiterate; unfortunately such a translation has stemmed from sheer ignorance.

(may Allāh be pleased with him) said that he could fill eighty camel loads of books just with the commentary of the *bā* of *Bismillāh*.[8] He could only say this if the Qur'ān is unbelievably rich in terms of meaning and interpretation. Imām al-Qurtubī (d. 671 AH/1272 CE) filled twelve pages in his *Tafsīr* (exegesis) just on *Bismillāh al-Rahmān al-Rahīm*. His commentary of *Sūrah al-Fātihah* covers over thirty pages. More recently, Allāma Ghulām Rasūl Sa'īdī (may Allah shower His mercy upon him) wrote over two-hundred pages of commentary on *Sūrah al-Fātihāh* alone, which only consists of seven verses.

In terms of Sharī'ah, the *Usūl al-Fiqh* scholars laid down tools to deduce rulings from the Holy Qur'ān. *Ibārat al-nass*, *ishārat al-nass*, *dalālat al-nass* and *iqtidhā al-nass* are examples of such tools. Here are two examples to show how a verse can reveal so much information:

2.3.1.

أُحِلَّ لَكُم لیلةَ الصیامِ الرفثُ الي نِسائِكم هُنَّ لِباسٌ لكم وانتم
لباسٌ لهنَّ عَلِمَ اللهُ اَنَّكم كُنتم تَختانونَ انفسَكم فتابَ عليكم و

8 Al-Sha'rānī reports that Alī (may Allāh be pleased with him) used to say: 'If I wished, I could fill eighty camels [worth of books] on the *bā* [from *bismillāh*]' (*Latā'if al-minan*, 1: 171).

عفا عنكم فالأن بٰشِرُوهنَّ وابتغُوا ما كتبَ اللهُ لكم وكُلُوا واشرَبُوا
حتي يَتبيَّنَ لكم الخيطُ الابيضُ من الخيطِ الاسودِ مِنَ الفجرِ

It is made lawful to you to have sexual relations with your wives on the night of fasts. They are clothing for you and you are clothing for them. Allah knows that you were deceiving yourselves [in this respect] so He accepted your penance and forgave you. So cohabit with them and seek what Allah has destined for you - and eat and drink until the white thread (of dawn) is clear to you from the black thread. Then complete your fasts till the nightfall.

(Qur'ān, 2: 187).

In its simplest form, we learn from this verse that Muslim couples are allowed to sleep with one another during the nights of Ramadān, and that they can eat, drink (and have sexual relations) right until the point of dawn.

But owing to the vastness of the Qur'ān and the scholars' expertise, we can also deduce the following:

a. That rinsing the mouth and cleaning the nose do not negate the fast. Because the couple can have sexual intercourse right until the last moment of dawn, it means the fast will commence in the state of impurity. So they are required to have a bath (*ghusl al-janāba*) once the fast has started. And rinsing the nose and mouth is obligatory in *ghusl*.

b. Tasting something with the mouth does not negate the fast. This is because as he/she has a bath, the water may be salty and he/she is legally required to rinse the mouth.

c. Having a wet dream (*iḥtilām*), applying oil and performing cupping also do not negate the fast. This is because the verse informs us that fasting is complete (*itmām*) when a person refrains from three elements; eating, drinking and sexual intercourse. So the fast is legally completed when a person completes the day having refrained from these three things.

2.3.2.

لِلْفُقَرَاءِ الْمُهَاجِرِينَ الَّذِينَ أُخْرِجُوا مِن دِيَارِهِمْ وَأَمْوَالِهِمْ

And there is also a share in this booty for
the poor emigrants, who were expelled
from their homes and their property...

(Qur'ān, 59:8).

In its simplest form, the verse indicates that the Emigrants (who migrated from Makka to al-Madīna) also have a right to the spoils of war, just like other Muslims. However, additional points can be deduced from this text. For example, they have been described as 'poor' in the verse. This proves – by the means of *ishārat al-nass*[9] – that as they left Makka, they were no longer the legal owners of the land, homes and wealth they left behind. If they were, then they would not be described as 'poor' in this verse. There are alternative terms used for people who own property elsewhere (in the Qur'ān), namely *ibn al-sabīl*, a wayfarer. So, the verse also proves the following points, by means of *ishārat al-nass*;

a. The non-Muslims in Makka became the legal owners of the property and wealth left behind by the Muslims.

b. If the non-Muslim wanted to sell the property and give it as a gift, he could, and if slaves were left behind by the Muslims, he could legally free them. If he sold the property to another trader, then he would become the legal owner.

c. If the same non-Muslim appeared again in the battlefield

9 *Ishārat al-Nass* is what is proven from the sacred text without any addition. It is hidden in all aspects and it is not the reason why the dialogue was delivered in the first place.

and left the property behind (e.g. a horse) and fled, then this property becomes classified as war booty, and the original owner does not necessarily have an automatic right over it.

d. If, after the division of war booty, a fellow Muslim becomes the owner of the property, the original owner cannot take it off him by claiming that it was his originally.

2.4. Conclusion

When Muslims constantly remind themselves that the Qur'ān is the word of Allāh, only then will they appreciate how much care and caution they should approach it with. When a scholar studies the Qur'ān in the correct manner and recites it repeatedly, then an ocean of knowledge opens up in front of him. The countless, reliable and lengthy exegeses written by the great scholars of the past is testimony to this very fact.

But when people with no scholarly background attempt to draw their own conclusions from the Qur'ān, the outcome is always misguidance. Typically, the extremist Muslims quote and misuse a verse out of its correct context, or fail to analyse the verse in light of other verses on the same subject. In short, *'By it [the Qur'ān] Allah misleads many and by it, He guides many'* (Qur'ān, 2: 26).

3.0. THE SUNNAH

3.1. The meaning of Sunnah

The literal meaning of Sunnah is 'path' or 'way'. In Islamic Sharī'ah, the term is used to denote the sayings, actions and tacit approvals of the Prophet ﷺ. For the purpose of our discussion here, this is the definition that will be applied. Otherwise, in the field of *fiqh* (jurisprudence), it is also used to classify an action. What this means is that when something is described as 'Sunnah', then it is not *fard*, *wājib* or *nafl*. Mighālwī defines this type of Sunnah as:

السنةُ تُطلقُ علي ماليسَ بِواجبٍ وقِيلَ هي ماواظبَ
الرسولُ ﷺ علي فعلِه مع تركِه في بعضِ الاحيانِ بلاعُذرٍ

Al-Sunnah is used to denote something that is not *wājib*. It is also said that it is something that the Prophet ﷺ did on a permanent basis, though he left it sometimes without reason.[10]

10 Mighālwī 1998, p. 120.

3.2. The relationship between the Qur'ān and Sunnah

The Sunnah is an indispensable part of Sharī'ah, not least because the words and actions of the Prophet ﷺ constitute a commentary and interpretation of the Qur'ān. Professor Abd al-Hayy describes the relationship between the Qur'ān and Sunnah as follows:

3.2.1. The Sunnah acts as a reminder of the Qur'ān. So, for example, when the Prophet ﷺ referred to the importance of *salāh*, he was emphasising what the Qur'ān had already outlined.

3.2.2. The Sunnah acts as an explanation of what the Qur'ān has outlined. For example, the Qur'ān instructs Muslims to perform *salāh* and it was the Prophet ﷺ who taught us the conditions, timings and method of *salāh*. The Qur'ān orders *zakāh* and it is the Sunnah that explains what needs to be given and how often.

The Sunnah (as an explanation of the Qur'ān) cannot be over emphasised because it is impossible to understand the Qur'ān without Prophet Muhammad ﷺ. No Muslim can act upon the teachings of the Qur'ān without referring to his ﷺ example, because he was the Qur'ān personified. Allāh did not merely send Prophet Muhammadﷺ to deliver the Qur'ān; his duty was to 'recite the verses of the Qur'ān, purify the people and teach them...' (Qur'ān, 3: 164). In short, the Qur'ān is a book that can only be read in the light, namely the *nūr* of Muhammadﷺ.

3.2.3. The Sunnah explains a matter of Sharī'ah that has not been mentioned in the Qur'ān. For example, the prohibition of marrying a woman along with her paternal/maternal aunt has no mention in the Qur'ān; this in fact stems from the Prophetﷺ. Likewise, a murderer is written out of the inheritance of the murdered. There is no mention of this in the Qur'ān. From this, we can appreciate the position of the Sunnah in Islām and that in places, it is an autonomous source of Sharī'ah.[11]

3.3. The authority of the Sunnah

The Qur'ān itself has stressed the importance of the Sunnah in numerous places. Here are just a few:

وَأَطِيعُوا اللَّهَ وَأَطِيعُوا الرَّسُولَ وَاحْذَرُوا

11 Abd al-Hayy 1998, pp. 124-5.

And obey Allāh and obey the Messenger and beware

(Qur'ān, 5: 92).

قُلْ أَطِيعُوا اللَّهَ وَأَطِيعُوا الرَّسُولَ فَإِنْ تَوَلَّوْا فَإِنَّمَا عَلَيْهِ مَا حُمِّلَ وَعَلَيْكُم مَا حُمِّلْتُمْ وَإِنْ تُطِيعُوهُ تَهْتَدُوا وَمَا عَلَى الرَّسُولِ إِلَّا الْبَلَاغُ الْمُبِينُ

Say [O Messenger]: Obey Allāh and obey the Messenger. And if you turn away, he is only responsible for the duty placed on him and you for that placed on you. If you obey him, you will be guided. The Messenger's duty is only to convey

(Qur'ān, 24: 54).

وَمَا آتَاكُمُ الرَّسُولُ فَخُذُوهُ وَمَا نَهَاكُمْ عَنْهُ فَانْتَهُوا وَاتَّقُوا اللَّهَ إِنَّ اللَّهَ شَدِيدُ الْعِقَابِ

And whatsoever the Messenger gives you, take it. And whatsoever he forbids you, abstain from it. And fear Allāh. Verily Allāh is severe in punishment

(Qur'ān, 59: 7).

مَنْ يُطِعِ الرَّسُولَ فَقَدْ أَطَاعَ اللَّهَ

He who obeys the Messenger

has indeed obeyed Allāh

(Qur'ān, 4: 80).

The Companions were unbelievably faithful to the Prophet's ﷺ Sunnah. They followed each and every one of his actions, religious or otherwise. In a hadīth, we are informed that the Prophet ﷺ once removed his blessed sandals. The Companions observed the Prophet's actions and they too removed their footwear. Upon seeing this, the Prophet ﷺ asked them why they removed their footwear, since he had not told them to do so. The Companions humbly replied that they were merely following his actions. The Prophet ﷺ replied: 'I removed my sandals because Jibrīl عليه السلام just came to me and informed me that there is something harmful in them.'

Another narration informs us that between Makka and al-Madīna, there was a specific tree. Whenever he passed by it, Ibn Umar (may Allāh be pleased with him) would sleep there for a while and then move on. When asked why, he said, 'I saw my Messenger ﷺ sleep under this very tree'.[12]

Despite their eagerness to emulate him, there were some practices that he ﷺ performed that were specific to him and

12 Al-Munzirī 2001, p. 20.

were not to be emulated by either his Companions or those after them. He clearly told his Companions about the status of such acts, like fasting continuously for several days (*sawm wisāl*).

People would come to Imām Mālik's[13] house for religious advice and guidance. If he was asked for a religious decree, then he would offer it immediately. If he was asked to report a hadīth then he would disappear into his house. He would only reappear and report one after having a bath, wearing new, clean clothes and applying perfume. Only then would he report a hadīth.[14] This certainly indicates how much honour early Muslims had for the Prophet's ﷺ Sunnah.

For each hadīth he included in his *Sahīh*, Imām al-Bukhārī[15] used to perform *istikhāra* prayer and two units of *nafl* prayers at the Prophet's ﷺ final resting place in al-Madīna before including each and every hadīth into his compilation. He did

13 Imām Mālik ibn Anas, (d. 179 AH). Major hadīth scholar and jurist of al-Madīna. He compiled the *al-Muwatta*, the hadīth collection deemed as one of the most authentic compilations by Imām al-Shāfi'ī. The Mālikī school of thought takes its name from him.

14 Al-Qādī Iyād 2002, p. 267.

15 Al-Bukhārī, Imām Muhammad ibn Ismā'īl (d. 256 A.H.). Compiler of *al-Jāmi al-Sahīh*, which is unanimously regarded as the most reliable of all the hadīth collections.

this at least four thousand times.[16]

3.4. Classifying the Sunnah

Although there are many different ways to classify the Sunnah, only three will be mentioned here:

3.4.1. Classification One

a. *Sunnah Qawliyya*: This means something the Prophet ﷺ said. For example, he famously said, 'Actions are judged according to intentions.'

b. *Sunnah Fi'liyya*: This describes an action of the Prophet ﷺ. How he performed *salāh*, Hajj and fasting are all examples of this type.

c. *Sunnah Taqrīriyya*: This is when an action was done in the presence of the Prophet ﷺ and he did not object to it. So his silence is in effect affirming its approval. This type derives directly from the Qur'ān and works on the notion

16 There are four thousand *ahādīth* in *Sahīh al-Bukhārī* without including the repetitions. Including the repeated reports, the number is 7275.

that a prophet would never remain silent when something wrong occurred in his presence. For example, when Mūsā (peace be upon him) saw al-Khizr kill a small child, he immediately spoke up and said: 'Have you killed an innocent person who had killed none?' (Qur'ān, 18: 74). In the time of Prophet Muhammad ﷺ, the Companions would practice the withdrawal method of contraception.[17] Ibn Umar (may Allāh be pleased with him) said that whilst the Prophet ﷺ was alive, they would describe Abū Bakr, Umar and Uthmān as the best men after Prophet Muhammad.[18] These are two examples of *Sunnah Taqrīriyya*.

3.4.2. Classification two: the division based on how accurately it reached us

In terms of legal weight, there is little to no difference between the Qur'ān and Sunnah. The only difference is in how it has reached us. With the Holy Qur'ān, it has been passed down

---

17 Mighālwī 2003, p. 498.
18 Mighālwī 2003, p. 498. Abd Allāh ibn Umar (may Allāh be pleased with him) said: 'We used to say - whilst the Messenger of Allāh ﷺ was alive - that the best of this Ummah after its Prophet is Abū Bakr, Umar and Uthmān. The Messenger of Allāh ﷺ would hear us and not object to it.' The origin of this report is to be found in *Sahīh al-Bukhārī* (The virtues of the Companions, the superiority of Abū Bakr).

in the most secure manner, with no room for doubt. With the Sunnah, there are different degrees of authenticity, owing to how securely it was passed down to Muslims. Some *aḥādīth* (sayings and actions of the Prophet ﷺ) are on par with the Qur'ān in terms of strength and some *aḥādīth* are either weak or even forged. In short, there are three categories:

a. *Al-Mutawātir*: This is a ḥadīth that was reported from the Prophet ﷺ by so many people that it is impossible that they all colluded on a lie, or all said the same thing coincidentally. Examples are wiping on the leather socks and the lifting of the hands during a *du'ā*.

c. *Al-Mashhūr*: This is a report that was first reported by a handful of Companions, but thereafter it was reported by so many Muslims that it becomes impossible to deny. In terms of ruling, it is below *al-mutawātir*. An example is the ḥadīth 'Actions are judged according to intentions.' This is a very famous ḥadīth, but only one Companion reported it from the Messenger ﷺ, namely Sayyidunā Umar (may Allāh be pleased with him). In the generations that followed him, it was reported *en masse*.

d. *Al-Āḥād* (or *Khabar al-Wāḥid*): This is a ḥadīth that

has been reported by less, sometimes just one or two individuals.

3.4.3. Classification three: whether it is acted upon or not

A hadīth may be considered as *sahīh* (authentic) but according to the scholars it may not be acted upon. There are many reasons for this, only three will be mentioned here.

a. The hadīth is abrogated (*mansūkh*). When an earlier ruling is replaced with a latter one, then this is called *nuskh*. For example, there was a time in Islām when visiting the graves was prohibited. Later, this was overturned. So the hadīth on preventing people visiting the grave is *sahīh* (authentic), but it is not acted upon. The same applies (according to the Hanafī school of thought) with (i) repeating *wudū* after eating something cooked directly on fire (ii) raising the hands in *salāh* (iii) saying *āmīn* loudly in congregational prayer.

c. The hadīth is specific to the Prophetﷺ. What this means is that the Prophetﷺ performed a certain practice but this was for him alone and his followers were not permitted to do the same. For example, there are plenty of authentic *ahādīth* which mention how the Prophet ﷺ married more than four women. This was specific to him. Other examples include performing *salāh al-janāza* (Funeral Prayer) when the body is absent. The Prophet ﷺ led the *salāh al-janāza* of al-Najāshī (the king of Abyssinia) though his body was not present. The hadīth on this is to be found in *Sahīh al-Bukhārī* but the Hanafīs do not act upon it. A third example is *sawm wisāl*, meaning keeping fasts continuously for many days. Again, this report is to be found in *Sahīh al-Bukhārī* but Muslims cannot perform *sawm wisāl*.

d. Because when there are multiple, contrasting reports on a given topic area, we give preference to the hadīth that has been reported by more skilled, learned individuals. The preferred one is called *mahfūz* and the other is called *shāz*.

3.5. Conclusion.

An observer who studies the Sunnah in detail will inevitably be astonished with the wisdom, guidance and intelligence of Prophet Muhammad ﷺ. Moreover, his advice and example was not specific to the field of religion alone - he provided so much insight into matters such as medicine, economics, politics and diplomacy. Like with the Qur'ān however, the interpretation of the Sunnah lies with the learned and skilled scholars, not with ordinary Muslims. The chances are that a casual reader may be subject to confusion rather than inspiration.

For instance, can Muslims perform two units of prayer before *maghrib* (sunset prayer)? On this issue, there are prophetic reports that suggest it is permissible *and* impermissible. Without the guidance of a skilled teacher, an ordinary Muslim can never reach the correct ruling. Another example is on the matter of *bid'a* (innovation). In one saying, Prophet Muhammad ﷺ outlawed all innovations as misguidance. Yet in another authentic report, he praised those who innovated a good innovation.[19]

The classical scholars knew that the vast ocean of Sunnah literature could cause confusion for ordinary Muslims. In order to prevent this from happening, they made hadīth compilations of prophetic reports specifically designed for the laypersons. A prime example is *Riyād al-Sālihīn* by Imām al-Nawawī (d. 676 AH/1277 CE). The *ahādīth* in this collection are inspirational yet easy to understand and comprehend. Until a Muslim masters Arabic grammar and the other Islamic sciences, compilations such as *Riyād al-Sālihīn* should be read.

19 Imām al-Nasā'ī reports in his *Sunan* from Jābir (may Allāh be pleased with him) that Prophet Muhammad ﷺ said: 'The worst matters are the innovated ones (*muhdathāt*) and every *muhdathāt* is *bid'a*. Every *bid'a* is misguidance and every misguidance is destined for the fire' (Book of Two Eids; Chapter, the Sermon). Similar authentic reports are to be found in *Sahīh Muslim*, *Sunan Ibn Mājā*, *Sunan al-Dārimī* and *Musnad Ahmad*. This hadīth seemingly suggests that Prophet Muhammad ﷺ declared all *bid'a* as misguidance. This is not the case, when we read other prophetic reports on the subject. A'isha (may Allāh be pleased with her) reports that Prophet Muhammad ﷺ said: 'Whoever innovates [something] that is not from our matter [of Islām] then it is rejected' (*Sahih al-Bukhāri*, Book of s*ulah*). This clearly indicates that not all *bid'a* is rejected but rather those that are alien to Islām. Similarly, Imām Muslim reports in his *Sahīh* that Jarīr ibn Abd Allāh (may Allāh be pleased with him) narrated that Prophet Muhammad ﷺ said: 'Whosoever initiates a good practice in Islām, then he will attain the reward for it and the reward of whoever acts upon it thereafter...' (Book of Knowledge). Again, this shows that not all *bid'a* is rejected. If this was the case, then he would never have promised a reward for those who initiate a good practice. This case shows that one has to have knowledge of all *ahādīth* on a subject matter before forming an opinion.

4.0. *IJMĀ* (SCHOLARLY CONSENSUS)

4.1. Introduction

In order to appreciate and understand *Ijmā*, one must remember that in Islām, the focal point is the Ummah (global Muslim community) and not the individual. In fact, the self has very little status. Consider the following points, all of which indicate the worth of *Ijmā*:

- Most of the Qur'ānic *du'ā*s commence with رَبَّنَا (our Lord) and not رَبِّي (my Lord). This indicates that we should keep everyone in mind in our *du'ā*s, not just ourselves. Incidentally, the *du'ā*s in the Qur'ān for knowledge begin with ربي . In other words, seeking knowledge is an individual responsibility not a collective one.

- Many forms of worship prescribed in Islām are collective or at least have the interests of all at heart. *Salāh* (prayer) can be read alone but male Muslims are encouraged to read collectively. *Zakāh* benefits all, especially the underprivileged. Fasting is a collective worship done by all at the same time.

- Laws passed in Sharī'ah always preserve the interests of the community as opposed to the interests of the individuals. This is why Islām is quite severe on crimes such as stealing and the consumption of alcohol. A whole street should not be deprived of sleep because of the evil of one thief. He should be punished rather than the whole community. Islām deals with the alcoholic alone rather than the multiple problems that arise when alcoholism is allowed to flourish.

- This is why emphasis is given to *shūra* (consultation) in Islām. Our Prophet ﷺ was taught directly by Allāh so he did not make incorrect decisions. Despite this, he still consulted with his Companions.

Therefore it is no surprise to learn that when all scholarly Muslims agree on a particular issue after the Prophet's life ﷺ then it has weight and value. This is what the *Ijmā* is.

4.2. The definition of *Ijmā*

Mighālwī[20] defines *Ijmā* as follows:

هُوَ اِتفاقُ المُجتَهدينَ مِنَ الأُمَّةِ الإِسلاميةِ فِي عَصْرٍ
مِنَ العُصُورِ علي حُكمٍ شَرعيٍ بَعدَ وَفاةِ النَّبِيِّ ﷺ

Ijmā is the consensus of the mujtahidūn
(practitioners of independent reasoning) from
the Muslim Ummah in a generation upon a
Sharī'ah ruling, after the time of the Prophet ﷺ.

From this comprehensive definition we can identify the following:

...consensus

The consensus must consist of all scholars of the time. Therefore, when the scholars of Makka and al-Madīna agree on something, then it does not necessarily give the opinion weight. Scholars of all areas of the Muslim world must be part of it.

20 Mighālwī 1998, p. 146.

...of the mujtahidūn

Ijmā is a scholarly consensus, not one of the laypersons. Only the opinion of the learned counts. In *Usūl al-Shāshī* it is stated:

والمُعتَبَرُ في هذا البابِ إجماعُ أَهلِ الرأي والاجتهادِ, فلا يُعتَبَرُ بقولِ العوامِ والمتكلمِ والمُحدِّث الذي لا بَصيرةَ له في أصولِ الفقه

And what is considered in this area is the consensus of the people of opinion and ijtihād. Thus there is no consideration for the opinion of laypersons, the ilm al-kalām experts or [even] the hadīth masters that have no insight in Usūl al-Fiqh.[21]

...from the Muslim Ummah

These scholars must be Muslims. There is no concept of an *Ijmā* involving non-Muslims. Also, the *Ijmā* has only been considered as a part of Sharī'ah for this Ummah, and not previous ones.

The *Ijmā* is a noble gesture which highlights the virtue of this Ummah. In the Qur'ān, Allāh describes this Ummah as the

21 *Al-Tashīl al-Kāfī Sharh Usūl al-Shāshī* 2005, p. 229.

'best of communities' (3:110). Also, the Prophet ﷺ said in a report recorded by Imām al-Tirmidhī that his Ummah would never agree on falsity.

...upon a Sharī'ah ruling

The consensus must be on a Sharī'ah ruling, not on a secular matter. Also, the *Ijmā* is only applicable to certain parts of Sharī'ah, namely peripheral matters (*furū*) rather than the core ones (*usūl*). The core parts of our religion – such as monotheism, the attributes of Allāh, belief in the hereafter and so on – have been conclusively proven and explained from the Qur'ān and Sunnah and therefore cannot be altered. If, for example, all the scholars in the world were to agree to shorten the fasts in Ramadān (till *asr* time, for example), then it would hold no weight whatsoever. This is because the timing of fasts is proven conclusively from the Qur'ān and Sunnah.

...after the time of the Prophet ﷺ

This consensus must happen after the Prophet ﷺ left this world. The reason is that during his lifetime there was no consensus, since the Muslims had his authority to resort to, who himself was the recipient of divine instructions.

4.3. The types of *Ijmā*

There are two types of *Ijmā*, *Ijmā Sarīh* and *Ijmā Sukūtī*.

a. *Ijmā Sarīh*: This is when the scholars apply a ruling together in words or actions.

b. *Ijmā Sukūtī*: This is when some scholars apply a ruling in words or actions and the others remain silent over it. The fact that they remain silent on it is in effect showing their approval.

4.4. What is the proof that *Ijmā* is one of the sources of Sharī'ah?

a. In the Holy Qur'ān, Allāh declares:

> *And whosoever opposes the Messenger after the right path has been shown clearly to him and follows other than the way of the believers, We shall keep him in the path he has chosen and burn him in hell; and what an evil destination'*
>
> (Qur'ān, 4: 115).

Here, Allāh promises the hell-fire for the one who opposes the Messenger ﷺ and the way of the believers. The way of the believers (note, plural) is what they have unanimously agreed upon.

b. The Prophet ﷺ said in a hadīth recorded by Ibn Mājā:[22]

إنّ أُمَّتِي لا تَجْتَمِعُ على ضلالةٍ

My Ummah shall never unite on misguidance.

Here, we are informed that when the Muslims unite on an issue, then it will not be on misguidance. Therefore their collective opinion is valuable in Islām.

c. The great Caliph Umar (may Allāh be pleased with him) wrote to his judges during his caliphate:[23]

اِقْضِ بِمَا فِي كتابِ اللهِ فَإِنْ لم يكنْ فبما سَنّه رَسُوْلُ
اللهِ فَإِنْ لم يكنْ فبما أَجْمعَ عليه الصَّالِحون

Decree according to the Book of Allāh.
If you do not find it here, then with the
Sunnah of the Messenger of Allāh ﷺ. And

22 *Sunan Ibn Mājā, kitāb al-fitan; bāb al-sawād al-a'zam.*
23 *Sunan Ibn Mājā, kitāb al-fitan; bāb al-sawād al-a'zam.*

if you do not find it there, then on what the pious (Muslims) have agreed upon.

d. In a hadīth recorded by Imām al-Tirmidhī in his *Sunan*,[24] the Messenger of Allāh ﷺ said that the 'hand of Allāh is on the *jamā'at* (majority).'

4.5. Examples of *Ijmā*

1. The prohibition of marrying grandchildren.[25] The Qur'ān outlaws the marriage to daughters and mothers (Qur'ān, 4:23). By consensus, it is also prohibited to marry granddaughters and grandmothers.

2. The paternal grandmother gets one sixth inheritance. This has been affirmed through the consensus of the scholars.

3. The caliphate of Sayyidunā Abū Bakr (may Allāh be pleased with him). All the scholars agree on the legitimacy of his caliphate, not least because during his lifetime, the Prophet ﷺ appointed him as the Imām in his absence.

---

24 *Sunan al-Tirmidhī, kitāb al-fitan; bāb mā jā fī luzūm al-jamā'at.*
25 Mighālwī 1998, pp. 152-3.

4. The addition of the second *azān* in the time of Sayyidunā Uthmān (may Allāh be pleased with him). All the Companions agreed with this because the Muslim population was increasing and there was a need to let them know the timing of *jum'a*.

4.6. Is an *Ijmā* still possible today?

There are opinions to suggest that in this day and age, it is almost impossible to enact a scholarly consensus on a matter of Sharī'ah. The advocates of this view say:

- The scholars are too scattered across the world and hardly meet.

- There is too much difference of opinion between the scholars in one country, let alone between numerous countries.

- There is no real agreement as to which scholars would be part of this consensus.

In reply, we must remember that the *Ijmā* is a source of Sharī'ah till the Day of Judgement and so Muslims must work to ensure it remains as such. In the past, the Pilgrimage (Hajj) acted as a conference for Muslims scholars of the world. Like with so many other areas of Islām, Muslims need to change their lifestyle and actions to suit Islām. Islām should not have to change to suit our lifestyle.

4.7. Conclusion

Symbolically speaking, the *Ijmā* reminds us that the opinion of many is better than the opinion of a few. A large part of the current crisis in the Muslim world is due to the fact that the opinion of a few has been forced on to everyone, without due deliberation and process. *Ijmā* teaches us that there is so much to be gained from working together as one, united Muslim Ummah. Spiritually speaking too, there are blessings to be gained from the companionship of one another too.

Implicitly, the *Ijmā* also serves to remind Muslims how knowledge is passed on by men and women of knowledge, not by books alone. The living tradition that connects Muslims today with their rich past is via a chain of transmission (*sanad*), consisting of learned men and women.

5.0. *QIYĀS* (LEGAL ANALOGY)

5.1. Introduction

Qiyās (legal analogy) is one of the four sources of Sharī'ah, although in rank, it is lower than the Qur'ān, Sunnah and *Ijmā*. Out of the four sources, perhaps this is the hardest to apply and therefore it is certainly the task of only the most skilled scholars and *mujtahids*.

When evidence cannot be located from the Qur'ān, Sunnah and *Ijmā* then it is necessary to act upon *Qiyās*. Like *Ijmā*, *Qiyās* cannot operate outside the framework of the Qur'ān and Sunnah.

Qiyās certainly indicates the brilliance of Sharī'ah. In particular, it is a tool that indicates how Islām can provide solutions and answers in the fast-changing world that we live in. New questions, scenarios, practices and circumstances that require an Islamic perspective are consistently appearing. *Qiyās* is the vehicle that allows us to provide answers in a dynamic and fast-evolving world.

5.2. The definition of *Qiyās*

5.2.1. Literal definition

Literally, *Qiyās* can have two meanings. One is that it means to 'measure something using something else'. For example a person may say:

قِسْتُ الثوبَ بالمترِ

I measured the cloth with a metre (stick).

The second meaning it can have is 'to be equal with something else', whether it is physical or otherwise. For example, a person may say:

فُلانٌ لا يُقاسُ بفلانٍ

Such and such cannot be compared
to such and such.

5.2.2. Terminological definition

القِياسُ الشرعِي هو تَرَتُّبُ الحُكمِ في غيرِ المَنصُوصِ عَليه
علىٰ معني هو علة لِذالك الحكمِ في المَنصوصِ عليه

Qiyās involves making a legal ruling by finding an established cause from an existing text (nass) and then applying it to an area where there is no existing text, through the means of a shared cause.[26]

There are four parts of this definition:

a. To affirm a legal ruling.

b. For a matter that does not have a textually established ruling.

c. Through one that does have a textually established ruling.

d. On the basis of a shared cause or meaning.

From a technical point of view, we learn that there are four central elements of this definition:

a. *al-Asl* (الأصل): The core. This means the ruling to be found clearly in the Qur'ān and Sunnah.

26 *Al-Tashīl al-Kāfī Sharh Usūl al-Shāshī* 2005, p. 253.

b. *al-Far'* (الفرع): The periphery. This means the ruling not to be found in the Qur'ān and Sunnah, though attempts are made to join it to the *asl*.

c. *Hukm al-Asl* (حكم الاصل): This is the formal ruling ascribed to the core.

d. *al-Illa* (العلة): This is the cause of the formal ruling.

5.3. Examples to explain what *Qiyās* is

5.3.1. Example I

Consuming alcohol is forbidden in Islām, through the Qur'ān and Sunnah. The legal cause (*illa*) for this prohibition is because it causes intoxication. In the Qur'ān and Sunnah, there is no mention of whether heroin is allowed or not. But we can do *Qiyās* with alcohol and make a ruling via this process. So we say that alcohol is forbidden because it causes intoxication and so heroin, which causes intoxication too, is also forbidden. We have reached this ruling via *Qiyās*.

Returning to the definition of *Qiyās*, we say *Qiyās* is:

a. To make a legal ruling (heroin is forbidden).

a. For a matter that does not have a textually established ruling (there is no mention of heroin in the sacred texts).

b. Through one that does have a textually established ruling (the prohibition of alcohol is mentioned in the sacred texts).

c. On the basis of a shared cause or meaning (both cause intoxication).

Great care has to be taken to ensure that a valid cause is derived. In the above example, an invalid cause would be alcohol is forbidden because it wastes valuable fruit. The correct cause is that it causes intoxication.

5.3.2. Example II

One can ask whether having a blood test is allowed during a fast. Clearly, because needles and syringes are relatively new, we will not find any direct reference in the Qur'ān and Sunnah. But the scholars have allowed it via *Qiyās*. They have stated that *hijāma* (blood-cupping) does not break the fast, which involves removing blood from the body. Also, being bitten by a mosquito does not break the fast either. Therefore, they deduce that injections too will not break the fast.

5.4. Proof for *Qiyās*

Qiyās is clearly proven from the Qur'ān and Sunnah. In fact, we learn that Prophet Muhammad ﷺ encouraged such analogous thinking. Here are just a few examples:

i. Mu'ādh ibn Jabal (may Allāh be pleased with him) was sent as a judge to Yemen by the Prophet ﷺ. When asked how he would make legal decisions, Mu'ādh affirmed that in the absence of evidence from the Qur'ān and Sunnah, he would do '*ijtihād*' (deep reasoning) with his opinion. The Prophet ﷺ congratulated him on his response.

   Ijtihād requires deep, intrinsic thinking as well as drawing analogies. Therefore the Prophet ﷺ sanctioned *Qiyās* as a source of Sharī'ah (27).[27]

27 *Al-Tashīl al-Kāfī Sharh Usūl al-Shāshī* 2005, p. 244.

ii. Ibn Abbās (may Allāh be pleased with him) reports that a man came to the Messenger ﷺ and asked, 'O Messenger of Allāh! My mother passed away and she had not performed one month's [obligatory] fasting. Shall I fulfil them on her behalf?' The Prophet ﷺ replied: 'If your mother had a debt to pay off, would you not pay it off?' He replied: 'Of course.' The Prophet ﷺ replied: 'The debt of Allāh is more deserved to be fulfilled'.[28]

In other words, the Prophet ﷺ compared a remaining monetary debt with the remaining fasts. Both have a shared cause. The Prophet ﷺ highlighted the *illa* (cause) to be found in each case. This is exactly what *Qiyās* involves.

iii. Once a man came to the Prophet ﷺ, and asked: 'O Messenger of Allāh! What is the opinion for when a person touches his private part after performing ablution?' He replied, 'Is it not but a part of the body?'[29]

The Prophet ﷺ here informed the man that the private part was simply a part of the body, just like the arms, feet and hands. If the ablution does not break from touching the

28 *Sahīh al-Bukhārī*, Book of Fasting; Chapter, Whosoever dies with fasts left to perform.
29 *Al-Tashīl al-Kāfī Sharh Usūl al-Shāshī* 2005, p. 245.

arms, how could it break from touching the private part? Again, the Prophet's ﷺ response was analogical in nature.

iv. In order to show the excellence of *salāh*, Prophet Muhammad ﷺ once asked his Companions their opinion of a person who bathed five times in a clean stream. When they remarked that such a person would have no impurities on his body, the Prophet ﷺ replied that *salāh* was similar; when a person performs *salāh* five times a day, then he is totally clean from minor sins.[30]

Again the Prophet ﷺ was drawing comparisons between two things, which is exactly what *Qiyās* entails.

5.5. The conditions for *Qiyās*

There are many important conditions that must be fulfilled before *Qiyās* is performed.

In *Uṣūl al-Shāshī*, the author explains that there are five such conditions:

30 Qārī 2007, II: 249.

(i) That the *Qiyās* is not contradictory to *nass* (i.e. sacred text from the Qur'ān and Sunnah).

(ii) That it does not lead to the changing of an existing ruling of the *nass*.

(iii) That the derived ruling is not based on a meaning contrary to common sense.

(iv) That the *Qiyās* has been done on Sharī'ah grounds, not lingual grounds.

(v) That *Qiyās* is not done to an area of Sharī'ah for which an existing ruling already exists.

Additionally, the scholars have stated that *Qiyās* cannot be done based on a one-off, unique example. For example, one Companion broke his fast and as a *kaffāra* (expiation), the

Prophet ﷺ allowed him to eat dates.[31] This cannot be used for *Qiyās* because it was a ruling specific to that Companion.

5.6. Conclusion

Muslims are living further and further away from the blessed era of the Prophet ﷺ and are facing an increasing amount of unprecedented Islamic queries. *Qiyās* is a wonderful tool that allows them to tackle new issues, through the flawless prism of Islām. Credit card transactions, share trading, modern medicine, transport and new technology are just a few areas for which Muslims have understood the Islamic perspective due to the application of *Qiyās*.

At the same time however, *Qiyās* cannot be treated as an

31 Abū Hurayra (may Allāh be pleased with him) reports: 'A man came to the Messenger of Allāh ﷺ and said: 'I am ruined O Messenger of Allāh! He replied: 'And what has brought about your ruin?' He replied: 'I had intercourse with my wife during Ramadān.' The Messenger asked: 'Can you find a slave to set free [as expiation]?' He replied: 'No.' The Messenger then asked: 'Can you observe fasts for two consecutive months?' He said: 'No.' He asked: 'Can you provide for sixty poor people?' He said: 'No'. The man sat down when someone brought a basket of dates to the Messenger. He said: 'Give these dates in charity.' The man replied: 'Am I to give this to one poorer than I? There is no family poorer than mine between the two lava plains of al-Madīna!' The Messenger of Allāh ﷺ laughed so much that his molar teeth became visible and said: 'Go and give it to your family to eat' (*Sahīh Muslim, kitāb al-siyām, bāb taglīz tahrīm al-jamā fi nahār Ramadān*).

exercise that can be performed by ordinary Muslims. A Muslim has to be aware of all the rulings from the Qur'ān and Sunnah that already exist, so that the *Qiyās* is done in a subject area that is covered by the sacred texts. From the prophetic sayings, one has to know which rulings are general and which ones were particular and specific to the Prophet ﷺ. The latter cannot be used for *Qiyās*. Similarly, there are countless other conditions that must be fulfilled before *Qiyās* can be performed. Clearly, this is the task of the learned scholars and not ordinary laypersons.

6.0. CONCLUDING REMARKS

The primary aim of this project has been to ensure people - Muslims and non-Muslims - warm to the term Sharī'ah. Due to a handful of extremists who have misused the term on television and radio, many non-Muslims fear for their lives when they hear the word. Then there are some Muslims in the UK who are hesitant to publicly declare their support for Sharī'ah, in case they are labelled extremists. Both sentiments are wrong. Just by a simple outline, I hope that readers have appreciated how brilliant yet complex Sharī'ah is. It is not something that should be feared, but something that should be studied properly and appreciated, with an open heart and mind.

For some Muslims, living one's life according to Sharī'ah is the ultimate goal in life. Anything less is considered sinful. In recent times we have seen Muslims become so insistent on applying Sharī'ah that they start performing illegal, un-Islamic acts in order to pursue this goal. Pursuing Sharī'ah whilst harming (and even killing) people is akin to mugging someone in order to donate to charity. If seeking this path leads to violence and ill-feelings towards others, then the object has been defeated. Such Muslims should understand that Sharī'ah is a path, leading to the real goal, the pleasure of Allah and Prophet Muhammad ﷺ. In the pursuit of obedience to God, one cannot display disobedience.

Then there are the Muslims who live in the West who truly believe that UK Law and Sharī'ah Law are incompatible. As a result, they have geared their efforts towards arguing that Sharī'ah in this day and age needs to change fundamentally or at least needs a rethink. These Muslims are the same ones who perhaps know least about Sharī'ah. Certainly they have totally overlooked the flexibility of it. For instance, although wearing silk is forbidden for Muslim men, Prophet Muhammad ﷺ allowed Zubayr and Abd al-Rahmān ibn Awf to wear silk due to an itchy skin condition they suffered from. During his caliphate, Umar (may Allah be pleased with him) temporarily suspended capital punishment because of a severe famine. Rather than highlighting the differences between Islamic and Western law, 'Reformists' Muslims today should consider highlighting the many similarities. They seem to forget that western law is in large parts based on ideas and concepts borrowed from Sharī'ah law. The underlying objectives of Sharī'ah (*Maqāsid al-Sharī'ah*) are not fundamentally different to modern day charters and constitutions. They seem to forget Islam is not contrary to common sense but in fact it is the greatest advocate of it.

Islam has never advocated a lifestyle for its followers that is difficult, unreasonable or damaging. It is up to Muslims in the UK to study the religion in more detail to actually appreciate this point. Once they do, they will realise they do not have to re-write the sacred texts, or dismiss its significance.

I hope this book has helped people to understand Sharī'ah. The more one understands an idea, the less fearful one becomes. More importantly, I hope it inspires readers to study this brilliant concept in further detail.

7.0. BIBLIOGRAPHY

Diyā Ilm al-Hadīth. Abū al-Irfān Muhammad Anwar Mighālwī. Ziā al-Qur'ān Publications, Lahore, Pakistan, 2003.

Mirqāt al-Mafātīh Sharh Mishkāt al-Masābīh. Mulla Alī Qārī (d. 1104 A.H.). Dār al-Kutub al-Ilmiyya, Beirut, Lebanon, 2007.

Sharh al-Waraqāt (al-Mahallī's notes on Imām al-Juwaynī's Islamic jurisprudence pamphlet). Imām al-Juwaynī al-Jalāl al-Mahallī (translation & notes by Musa Furber). Islamosaic Publications, 2014.

Al-Shifā. Abū al-Fadl Qādī Iyād ibn Mūsā ibn Iyād (d. 544/1149). Dār Ibn Hazm, Beirut, Lebanon, 2002.

Al-Targhib wa al-Tarhīb min al-Hadīth al-Sharīf. Al-Imām al-Munzirī. Dār ibn al-Hazm, Beirut, Lebanon, 2001.

Al-Tashīl al-Kāfī Sharh Usūl al-Shāshī. Abū Zafar al-Qādī Muhammad Ayyūb. Ziā al-Qur'ān Publications, Lahore, Pakistan, 2005.

Usūl al-Fiqh al-Muyassar. Dr. Abd al-Hayy Azb Abd al-Alllāh (al-Azhar University), 1999.

Al-Wusūl ilā al-Usūl fī Usūl al-Fiqh. Abū al-Irfān Muhammad Anwar Mighālwī, Ziā al-Qur'ān Publications, Lahore, Pakistan, 1998.